Distinctly Different

A Look at <u>God's Men</u>

<u>Leader's Guide</u>

By Carlton L. Coon Sr.

Leader's Guide for God's Men: Distinctly Different

By: Carlton Coon, Sr.

Copyright – 2018 by Carlton L. Coon Sr.

Unless otherwise noted quotations are from the King James Version of the Bible.

Editing: Pam Eddings
Graphics: Jolynn Mills

ISBN-13: 978-1724600431

ISBN-10: 1724600435

Printed in the United States of America

Leader's Guide

Contents

Thank you for being willing to help other men discover that they can be *Distinctly Different*. It does require a dedication of time for commitment and preparation to lead a group of men. It is my prayer that your time with the group of men will result in them having a further level of dedication and wise decision making.

Distinctly Different is the first in a series of books titled God's Men. Each book and chapter will focus on the issues with which Christian men have to deal.

What the Leader Needs to Know

Distinctly Different has seven chapters. Each chapter becomes a session dealing with the decision(s) of a man found in the Bible. You will need to make some decisions about how you will approach the material.

This leader's guide to *Distinctly Different* has more options than what you can use in a reasonable time frame. A reasonable time frame is 45- 60 minutes. The varied suggestions are offered because every group is different as is each leader.

Before your meeting, do the following:

1. Re-read the chapter being dealt with in this particular session.
2. After reading the chapter, consider the outcome you desire for the group you are leading through *Distinctly Different*.
3. Look at the various points of the application as a way to define the outcome. In some instances, you may want to develop personal points of application. Feel free to make the material in *Distinctly Different* and the *Leader's Guide to Distinctly Different* your own. The material is intended to be a tool.
4. Mark or highlight the parts of the leader's guide you will use to move the group toward the desired outcome. <u>Expect surprises!</u> Respond to them with grace, graciousness and if proper – good humor.
5. As you review the points of discussion, think about the answers with which men may come up.
6. If you use the material with a handout, create handouts as needed.

Begin every meeting with prayer. During each session there may be times when the Holy Ghost ministers in a special way. Give room for the spirit to work.

If food is part of the session, it is best to do food before or after rather than intermittently.

Leader's Responsibilities

1. **Love and encourage the men.** People are more receptive to truth and to being influenced by a leader who demonstrates an active love toward them.
2. **Let the material teach.** You are the leader. Do your best to relax and let the material work. However, your expertise will be needed to facilitate and cultivate good conversation. If a session does not go as well as you'd like – blame it on my material!
3. **Understand the benefits and dynamics of a group.** Interaction is vital for learning. *Do not do all the talking*. Instead facilitate the conversation. Try to establish an environment where each man has the freedom to express himself and ask questions.

Preparing to Start

1. Pray about the meeting and the men – before the meeting.
2. Organize for the session before the day of the meeting. If you are scurrying at the last minute you will seem to be ill-equipped to lead.
3. Prepare the room for the meeting. Again, have the room ready before a single man shows up.

Leading Your Group

1. Begin with prayer. End with prayer.
2. Be yourself. If men feel you are real they will be more willing to be genuine.
3. Structure your time. Set a time frame for dealing with each question or the leader's setup material. Stick with the schedule.
4. Contact the men to remind them of the event.
5. Support your pastor and church.

God's Men is a series focused on the issues of Christian men. The first in the series, *Distinctly Different* uses Bible characters in their unique situations to gain insight for living life today.

The leader's guide is intended to help a pastor, men's ministry leader or group leader help a group of men to gain full benefit. Some people do not enjoy reading. With that in mind, *Distinctly Different* is available as an audiobook at CarltonCoonsr.com or Audible.com.

A foolish person never learns. Such a man does not learn from his own mistakes. Nor does he learn from the mistakes of others.

Wise men gain wisdom from personal experience. Those who have great wisdom gain wisdom by learning from other men's experience.

Men are a vital key to an effective church. Thank you for investing in men.

Carlton L. Coon Sr.

Session 1
God's Men – Have a Long View

(<u>Note to Leader:</u> In each session, the opening will aim to get your group interacting in some way. Do your best to involve as many men as possible. Don't overlook newcomers to the church or young men. Their involvement is important for them to be interested in the content. The opening is designed to be a hook to hold interest.)

Tomorrow comes quick! Ready or not, each of us will soon have a birthday marking you as being 30 or 70. Some men can only see the immediate tomorrow. Other men realize the need to prepare for the long-term "tomorrows."

Discussion: What are the wrong approaches you see men taking toward the future? Can you connect those "wrong approaches" with a Bible principle even if you cannot quote the verse or cite its location?

Different Bible passages offer different views of the future.

<u>Note to Leader regarding the previous discussion:</u> _Distinctly Different_ referenced (1) Matthew 6:34: we are not to fret about the future. (2) Luke 14:28-30: living with no plan for the future. Jesus did not teach us to fail to save for retirement; fail to get an education or learn a trade.

Leader's Setup (Use to set up the next section): Most things of value do not happen overnight. They require a long-term effort in the same direction.

You don't buy a fiddle today
and play in Carnegie Hall tomorrow.
Charles Kettering

Some major corporations have a CEO who spends over 90% of their time on projects that will not bear fruit until five years in the future. Such men are always looking toward tomorrow.

Discussion: Does a person come to mind who is an example of what we just discussed? What has been the outcome for the person having prepared for the future?

Note to Leader regarding the prior discussion: It may be easier to think of someone who did not prepare. If the group struggles to find positive examples have them talk about someone who did not prepare. *Caution them not to use anyone's name.*

Esau and Jacob

Note to Leader: Have someone tell the story of Esau and Jacob's birth. It is best to have asked them a day before the session starts. Let them know you want it to be a quick recitation of no more than one minute.

Discussion: As the two grew up they were quite different. What do you recall about the brothers' differences?

Esau's Privilege

Leader's Setup (Use to set up the next section): Esau being older was significant. Being first-born was more than being known as the oldest.

- The eldest son received a double portion of their dad's inheritance.

- The eldest son would replace his father as head of the family.

- In pre-priesthood days, the father served as priest of the family.

The Old Testament term for this is called the *birthright*. In the family of Issac, the birthright had great significance. God had promised Esau's grandfather, Abraham, a particular piece of land and to make a great nation from his descendants. God's promise would flow to someone descended from Abraham. The eldest son, Esau was in line to benefit from the promise God made to Abraham.

While Isaac lived, the birthright had little significance for Esau. The birthright's value was attached to an unknown date in the future.

10

<u>A patient man would eventually gain great benefit from the birthright.</u>

Impatience is Dangerous

Few people *suddenly* find success. Being effective is the result of a long process. Some men want what they want – now!

<u>Discussion:</u> How have you seen impatience, perhaps to own a certain thing, affect a man? What are the areas where men easily lose patience?

Note to leader regarding prior discussion: Things to mention if someone else does not: (1) buying on credit rather than saving for a gun, boat or sports car. (2) Being sexually intimate prior to getting married. (3) Taking shortcuts in building something.

Unlikeable Jacob

We have talked a bit about Esau and his birthright. We have not talked a lot about Jacob. Jacob would be easy to dislike.

<u>Discussion:</u> Which of Jacob's actions would have caused you to dislike or not trust him?

Note to Leader: If necessary remind your group of Jacob's manipulation; tricking his father to gain a blessing intended for Esau. They may not know of Jacob's poor relationship with his in-laws. They may not have thought of Jacob as hiding behind his wife and children.

<u>Discussion:</u> Have you done business with a man like Jacob? What was the outcome? Would you do more business with that person? Why?

Jacob would have been easy to dislike. Our dislike of Jacob is immaterial; God's view is what matters.

But . . . God Loved Jacob

<u>Note to the leader.</u> Have Romans 9:13 read.

Leader's Setup: At times, we all act in ways others dislike. A great message of the Bible is God's love when we are not very lovable.

So, God loved Jacob. What does God see beyond Jacob's obvious misdeeds? What is the difference between Esau and Jacob that caused God to declare, "Jacob have I loved and Esau have I hated?"

Esau Lived for Today

Note to Leader: Recap, or have someone recap the story of Jacob and Esau to this point. (twins, quite different, competitive, Esau's birthright)

Note to Leader: Have someone tell the story of Esau selling his birthright. Ask them to tell the story in two minutes. (Genesis 25:30-34)

Discussion: What did Esau gain? What did he lose? Have you ever seen a man make such a bad trade? Why would anyone make such a trade?

Note to Leader: Have someone read Mark 8:36.

Setup: No man can gain the whole world. If we would not trade our soul for *the whole world*, why trade our soul for a tiny slice of this world?

Discussion: What are some actions of your peers that remind you a bit of Esau's bad deal?

Note to Leader: If you have access to a white board or flip chart write out the following words: **Esau despised his birthright**.

Setup: Esau *disesteemed* his birthright. *Disesteem* is the opposite of *esteem*. Instead of holding the birthright in high regard, the birthright had little consequence to Esau. Consider this. There is no evidence that Jacob tricked Esau!

Selling the birthright reflected Esau's values:

(1) Esau disesteemed the birthright.

(2) Esau lived for feeling good today.

This sense of values gave God reason to say, ". . . Esau have I hated." Jacob valued the birthright's benefit for tomorrow. Esau did not.

For God's purpose in the building up of the chosen people, Jacob the methodical and far-seeing,
was more suited than Esau the freelancer,
the rover, the child of impulse and passion.[1]
(F.B. Meyer)

Points to Make: Four Things To Consider Before Making a Trade

(1) Weigh the consequences the choice will make on your family's long-term well-being

(2) Does the decision reflect the values found in God's word?

(3) How tired, depressed or lonely are you? Ask yourself, "Am I acting impulsively?" Tired, hungry men make bad choices.

(4) To what appetite is this decision a response? Is the action I'm about to take a proper godly response to that appetite?

Long-Term Jacob

Leader's Wrap-up: Jacob had a long view. He repeatedly showed patience. He worked fourteen years to marry Rachel. Would you have done that?

Jacob did not expect a quick return on his investment of a bowl of lentil soup. He knew that in time there would be a great benefit.

Some men live only for today. They float on the river of life.

Jacob esteemed the birthright. He wanted to participate in what God was about to do. God needs men who live beyond today.

---

[1] Meyer, F.B., Great Verses Through the Bible; Zondervan Publshing, Grand Rapids, Michigan; p. 416.

Discussion and Application

Note to Leader: Application is important. Guide the group to apply what has been discussed. You may feel to pray **before** starting this part of the lesson.

1. What is your bowl of red pottage? The thing for which you'd trade a valuable future. Make no mistake, "red pottage" is always available. If you are willing to trade the meaningful for the meaningless, satan will arrange a trade. What relatively meaningless thing could get your attention? Know yourself and you thus protect yourself!

2. Is what you value more closely aligned with Esau or Jacob? Esau valued what he wanted now, more than God's plan for the future. Which do you most value?

3. Tired men make bad choices. Can you think of a regrettable decision you made when you were tired or in despair? What will you do to keep yourself from making a similar mistake in the future?

Session 2
God's Men - Failure Is Not Final

Discussion: Have men tell of a memorable success.

Setup for Leader: Men love talking about great victories. Ask, "Now who wants to tell us about a terrible failure?" Things usually get quiet when we begin talking about failure.

We do not celebrate failure. However, every man has failed! The man beside you has failed. As has the man you look at in the mirror each day.

Some allow failure or two failures to define their entire life. <u>They shouldn't</u>.

William A. Ward observed:

> Failure should be our teacher, not our undertaker . . .
> Failure is a delay, not defeat . . .
> Failure is a temporary detour, not a dead-end street.

Distinctly Different told of John Wooden introducing the fast break to basketball. At first the team did not fare well, but eventually Wooden's UCLA team won numerous national championships.

Discussion: Coaches are under pressure to win. Wooden stayed the course as he prepared his team to succeed. In the face of early failure, what other options do you think Wooden could have taken?

What Failure Looks Like

Note to leader: Quickly tell the story of John Mark leaving the first missionary journey. Acts 13 is the passage.

Discussion: As a boy, what was your response when someone called you a quitter? Why?

Leader's setup: John Mark quit. There is no other way to describe it. To worsen matters, John Mark was a well-connected young man.

- John Mark may have been the young man who followed along after Jesus arrest.
- Barnabas, Mark's uncle, was a great influencer.
- While Peter was in prison, the prayer meeting for his release was at the home of Mark's mother.

John Mark had great opportunity and privilege.

Discussion: Have you known a man who failed in spite of being born into privilege? Perhaps the family was well-to-do. In spite of this the son failed. What were the things that caused those men to fail?

Teaching Point: Connections give opportunity; connections do not assure success. Eventually, each man must establish his credibility.

Discussion: Imagine being Mark returning. How would you have felt? Be honest. What would your attitude be?

Discussion: Imagine being part of the church in Antioch. There was a great send-off for the missionaries. In a few weeks Mark returns. What do you think the talk would have been?

Leader's setup: Read Acts 15:37-38 about Barnabas' desire to take John Mark on another journey.

Discussion: Why do you suppose Paul was so adamant not to include Mark?

Teaching Point: God forgives, people forgive, and people remember. Paul may have been concerned working with a quitter! Can we blame Paul?

Leader's setup: John Mark has now failed as a missionary. He has been the cause of angry words between two great men. John Mark's failure would have been revisited in conversations among the saints.

Those who fail, whether it is their fault or not, often suffer silent contempt. Such situations become a topic for conversation. John Mark could have become a permanent loser.

John Mark is not heard of again till 2 Timothy 4:9-11. (Read the verse.)

Teaching opportunity: John Mark was now *profitable* to the man who would not go on a second missionary trip with him. He who had <u>been</u> a failure <u>became</u> profitable.

Discussion: The Bible does not give us the path of John Mark's life. It is clear, Mark became something different than what he had been on the first missionary journey. What might have been the essential steps in John Mark's becoming "profitable?"

Teaching opportunity: The starting point of success is obvious. John Mark did not quit! Whatever your failure or struggle – do not quit!

Teaching opportunity: (This portion of the lesson is important because recovery and restoration can be misunderstood. Men often want a "quick fix.") Many men want instant recovery. To immediately be trusted. It helps to understand the timeline of events in Mark's life.

- Paul, Barnabas and Mark go on a missionary journey.
- Six months into the trip – Mark quits.
- Eighteen months later, Paul and Barnabas return.
- A year later, Paul and Barnabas argue over John Mark. The two men separate.
- Seventeen years after the disagreement between Paul and Barnabas, Paul is in prison. He writes to Timothy and asks for Mark who would be "profitable."

Teaching Opportunity: Paul's words of affirmation are a total of eighteen and ½ years after Mark had quit. Eighteen years, not eighteen days, and not eighteen months. Eighteen years.

Discussion: Recovery starts immediately, but broken trust is slowly regained. Through seventeen years of which we know nothing, Mark had been consistent. Paul had heard good things about Mark's work. If you had been Paul what would you have needed to hear to restore your confidence in John Mark?

Teaching Opportunity: Mark's recovery wasn't high profile. Recovery from failure does not happen on a platform or in a leadership role. Recovery from failure is carried out by:

- Praying is vital. A man must have an ongoing commitment to prayer.
- Faithful service to your church, community and leaders.
- Consistent church attendance.
- Not getting an attitude about how long it takes to be again trusted.

Mark's profitability was a product of God's grace, an encouraging uncle, and Mark's diligent service. The first two were essential. However, without Mark's diligent service, there would have been no recovery. Mark would never have been spoken of as "profitable."

Wrap-up: Failure is not final. However, regaining trust and becoming profitable will take time.

Note to leader: Have your men pray for each other about how to respond to failure.

Application

1. After a failure, what response did you choose to make? If you have not shown consistency and steadfastness make a commitment to God and your leader today!
2. When you have failed either publicly or privately, what are your feelings? I'm not talking about what we portray to the public; I mean the feelings within.
3. As you consider others who have failed, how might you become the Barnabas, who gives them another opportunity?

Session 3
God's Men - Folly Is Not Their Legacy

Overview: This session is different. It looks at Abner, who took a wrong course. Abner was a contemporary of King David. The goal is to learn from Abner's mistakes to not repeat them.

Leader's Setup: In the Bible, over 2/3 of the uses of the word "fool" are in the wisdom literature of Proverbs and Ecclesiastes.

Perhaps to truly know wisdom, which is the goal of Proverbs and Ecclesiastes you must be shown a fool!

Discussion: When you think of the word "fool" what comes to mind? Why does that sort of person or behavior come to your mind?

Leader's Setup: Read 2 Samuel 3:33. Draw attention to: **"Died Abner as a fool dieth?"** To learn what prompted David to ask this, we will take a journey through Abner's life.

Note to Leader: Have a man tell about Abner's successes and impact. Ask for it to be three minutes in a bullet point approach. If some major information is left out, you will need to fill in the blanks.

Discussion: Consider Abner's abilities, influence and successes. Link those to David's closing comment, where he calls the man a "fool." How might a man go from being wonderfully successful to such a failure?

Teaching Point: No man is ever so successful as to not act foolishly. Every man can be a fool, regardless of past accomplishments.

Leader's Setup: Explain 2 Samuel 3 where Abner moves his allegiance from Saul's son, Ishbosheth, to David. (Refer to *Distinctly Different* if necessary.)

In his resentment of Ishbosheth, Abner offered to deliver eleven tribes of Israel to David. (2 Samuel 3:12, 17-21) David and Abner reached an agreement.

Brainstorming Discussion: Men, let's develop a list of behaviors we would label as foolish. When a behavior is added to the list, explain why the behavior is foolish. *(If possible have a marker board or flip chart on which to collect the words with which the group comes up. So you can keep the conversation moving, have someone else write the words in large letters. Let this discussion run for a bit. The group will be teaching and learning from each other.)*

Leader's setup: We don't have time to address each item. We will talk about Abner's folly. We can see the many paths to foolishness. The behavior that caused Abner to be labeled a fool may not connect with you. However, we will keep the list up because the behaviors on our list can have the same outcome.

(If nobody mentioned *over-reacting* or *lack of self-control* add those to the list.)

Leader's setup: Have someone tell the story or read the two passages telling the story of Abner killing Asahel. (2 Samuel 2, 2 Kings 2)

Discussion: What were the contrasts between Abner and Asahel? We will learn that Joab, Asahel's brother, believed Abner deserved to die for having killed his brother. The event might be termed "manslaughter."

Looked at from that perspective, how might Abner have dealt differently with Asahel? *(This can be difficult. If necessary, prod the group to consider Abner's expertise contrasted to Asahel. Asahel was a novice. Abner could best him. Abner held nothing back. Abner destroyed Asahel. In the heat of the moment, Abner lost control of himself.)*

Note to leader: *This scenario, may draw push-back from some. In response, remind them; Joab believed Abner a "man-slayer." The equal is modern day manslaughter. Don't belabor this or spend time arguing the matter.*

Leader Setup: You may be familiar with the Old Testament provision of "cities of refuge." *Have someone in the group prepared to explain the cities of refuge. They need to do it in two minutes.*

Leader's setup: Cities of refuge were provided for someone like Abner. In a city of refuge, Abner would be protected from Joab's revenge.

Discussion: Abner found refuge in Hebron. Where do men now find refuge from guilt and past mistake? *(This is a simple question, the discussion brief.)*

Leader's note: Have Hebrews 6:18-19 read. Refer back to the list of foolish behaviors. None here may need refuge for the same thing as Abner, but it is likely that we all need a refuge from at least one thing on the list.

<u>Lead the group in prayer that every man can find and live in God's shelter.</u> The time of prayer may become a "God-moment" where the Holy Ghost works. If a "God moment" happens let the spirit minister. You may also have men pray in groups of two or three.

Discussion: In Hebron, Abner was in a protected place. What might Abner have disliked about living in Hebron? *(Note to leader: remind the group; Hebron's primary residents were priests and Levites. Such men would have had a set of interests different from Abner. The situation was right to be frustrating for Abner. A man wallowing in frustration and self-pity is positioned for folly.)*

Discussion: If the church is a safe place for overcoming a man's past, why do some have difficulty staying in that "safe place?" Do you suppose some men have an incorrect perception of the "manliness" of devoted Christians? How could we change how men see being "in the church?"

Leader's setup: Have someone quickly tell the story of Abner foolishly leaving the place of refuge.

Discussion: Put yourself in Abner's shoes. What may have prompted Abner to step outside Hebron?

Leader's Recap

What steps led to Abner dying as a fool dieth?

- *No impulse control.* In killing Asahel, Abner did not constrain his abilities. A lack of self-control can be the start of folly.

- *The place of refuge was safe, but not comfortable.* Godly men are different in behavior from those with whom a man used to party.

- *The walls of Hebron constrained Abner's natural inclinations.* The Bible offers specific rules for life, and a pastor often directs men to live within certain safe boundaries.

- *Improper assumptions.* Abner assumed Joab's motives were safe. Foolish men assume. Such assumptions are often wrong. What would a man do if he <u>knew</u> his action would have a negative outcome?

Final Discussion: What could have kept Abner from being labeled a fool? Apply that us. What should we do to keep from being labeled a fool?

Thoughtful Consideration and Application

1. What is your response when things go wrong? Do you over-react? How could you slow impulsive behavior and think about your response?

2. What things about church life that don't always fit your male identity?

3. How could men within our church create a better comfort zone for men to realize that God's men are manly?

Session 4
God's Men – Seek True Success

Success has made a failure of many a man!

Leader's Setup: Tell the story of Johnny Devoe. If you have a personal illustration it would be better to use your story. Be sure your story makes the same point.

Discussion: Is Johnny Devoe (or the man in your story) a success? If what Johnny attained is not success why are many men chasing those exact things?

Leader's setup: The statement, "He who has the most toys wins," is foolish. Success can be a man's undoing. American President Woodrow Wilson called it, "... being defeated by your secondary successes."

Discussion: What are things you have seen men pursue, to the point of excluding almost everything else from their life?

Teaching Point: The things you mentioned are often not good or bad. The problem comes when a man cannot balance his desire to collect guns or gain a doctoral degree with the great value found in other things.

Discussion: Let's talk about us and our goals. What drives us? *(Note to leader: If not mentioned, insert the idea of men who are driven by events of childhood and how others have treated them.)*

Leader's Setup: The story of Jephthah is only a few verses. *(Note to leader: Tell the story or read the verses. If you do the latter, pause long enough to explain and draw attention to what is happening in each verse.)*

Leader's Setup: Tell the story of Jephthah's commitment regarding sacrifice and the outcome that involved his daughter.

Discussion: Do you see any of Jephthah in yourself or at some point earlier in life? What do you think of Jephthah's blind commitment? His ambition to succeed, particularly with this particular thing?

Teaching Point: His father and the elders had not valued Jephthah. Jephthah's siblings had disrespected him. Two generations had not appropriately valued Jephthah. <u>But now, Jephthah carelessly sacrificed the generation that followed him on the altar of his success</u>. Is there anything you do that sacrifices the arriving generation? Do you suppose Judge Jephthah, would say, "My success was worth what it cost me?"

Discussion: What could Jephthah have done differently? (Let your men talk about it. *Distinctly Different* has some suggestions.)

Teaching Point: Are you pursuing success or pleasure at the cost of your family? Be honest. If you do this, your children will pay. Please reevaluate what matters. Don't follow Johnny Devoe and Judge Jephthah into a success that is a defeat.

Discussion: Do you know someone driven to have certain "things," because during childhood their family never had those "things?" What lengths have you seen a man go to to accomplish what he wants? How is a man who is trying to impress others a danger to himself and to his family?

Leader's setup: Abraham Maslow created a pyramid of human need. *(Note: You may want to put this on a screen or marker board. Pictures of Maslow's pyramid are readily available online.)*

1. The base of the pyramid is our need for food, drink and a place to live.
2. A step above is the need to have a sense of security. A safe place for himself and the man's family.
3. Maslow's third level on the pyramid is the need to belong.

Discussion: How have you seen men pursue the need to belong? *(Note: Some to mention, if others do not: playing on a sports team, being the biggest fan of a team, college fraternities, motorcycle clubs, Masonic lodges, Men's Health Clubs, owning an expensive car or house, country club membership, aggressive participation in politics, advanced degrees, or involvement with "Save the Whales, etc.)*

Leader's Setup: Abraham Maslow's fourth level of the "hierarchy of need" is *esteem needs*. Such a need is the need to be honored and have a sense of accomplishment. Not only do men want to "belong." Men want others to recognize that they belong and have accomplished meaningful things.

Discussion: What are some of the outcomes caused by men needing to be esteemed? *(Note to include:* (1. When unable to gain the needed esteem in the right places, men may seek it in unhealthy places. (2. Being obsessively driven. (3. Competitiveness. More is in *Distinctly Different*)

Teaching Point: Have you ever been guilty of pursuing something to the point that it was unhealthy? Unfortunately, a man's aggressive pursuit of belonging and esteem can be contrary to God's will.

Leader's Note: Be sensitive to the spirit. There may be men who suddenly see themselves. If you sense this, lead the men into prayer. It may be a good time to guide them to repentance.

Leader's Option: Consider going over, "A Pastor's List of Successful Failures" as found in *Distinctly Different*. Some items may warrant emphasis.

Thoughtful Consideration and Application

1. What in your childhood might serve as an unhealthy prod to drive you to attempt risky things to be seen as a winner?

2. What are the areas in which you are at the greatest risk of becoming a successful failure?

3. We all need affirmation. At the same time, we also are the providers of affirmation. What young man or child could you begin to encourage and affirm?

4. What three things could you change this week, that might keep you from going in the direction of sacrificing your child(ren) on the altar of your success? Of the three things, select one to do differently, beginning today.

Session 5
God's Men – Don't Pass on Their Pain!

Leaders Setup: Fathers can easily weigh in on the opening discussion question. Those not fathers will have to use their imagination.

Discussion: What things do you see as most difficult for a father?

Leaders Setup: A genogram examines the past few generations of a family. It does seem that addiction, abuse, physical maladies or depression flow from one generation to another.

A simple example of a genogram is your doctor having you complete a form that asks about your parents' past health. There is a correlation between history and you dealing with the same health challenge.

You will have seen this played out in people around you. <u>Not only does it happen physically, but it also happens spiritually as well</u>.

Information about the descendants of Max Jukes and Jonathan Edwards is in *Distinctly Different*. Read or tell what the researchers discovered.

Fathers make a difference. A man who thinks it works for him to say to his kids, "Do as I say, not as I do," fools himself.

Discussion: When you hear the phrase, "Abraham, Issac, and Jacob" what comes to mind?

Note to Leader: (Toss this out for contemplation, but be cautious about making it a discussion. What we want men to contemplate here may be stressful and resurrect forgotten resentment and anger.) Contemplate this: How do you wish your father had been a bit different?

Discussion: How might a father bring pain to a child's life? How can a father bring benefit to a child's life?

Leaders' Setup: Some men are set up for failure. Some of these manage to live in a way that changes things for their descendants. The goal of this session is helping to develop a strategy to intentionally be a positive influence on those who come after you.

Jabez is an example of this. Jabez did not get a good start in life. The name Jabez means, "he will cause pain." His mother named him this because she bore him in sorrow. Jabez' mom, experienced pain but the name she gave him was an unfortunate prophetic declaration regarding the child's future.

Discussion: Imagine having been named, "He will cause pain." Do you suppose the name would have made life easier or more difficult? In what ways might the name, Jabez, have complicated a child's life?

Note to leader: You know your group. If the song "A Boy Named Sue" referenced in *Distinctly Different* is something your men would identify with, use it by referring to the book. Otherwise bypass it.

Leader's Setup: You have heard, "Sticks and stones may break my bones, but words will never hurt me." That statement is not true. You need to know that YOUR words are powerful for good or bad. No word is empty of meaning. Few words have a limited life-span. The words used with family and others can bless or cause pain.

Discussion: What wounding phrases have you heard men use in speaking to their children or others? Why would a man speak words that wound? (<u>Note to leader:</u> Add to the list that a man is not thinking before he speaks; letting emotion drive him; anger at some other aspect of life; being a bully. The goal: to help men see themselves.)

Discussion: Can you remember a time when someone, perhaps your father, a coach or teacher spoke in a way that belittled you? What did the person say? How did you feel? Why did the words from that person create that particular response?

Teaching Point: If you remember those cutting words, it is certain they left a negative impact on you. Why say things that leave someone else feeling the same way? Some say, "I hated the way my dad talked to me. Now I find I'm becoming just like my dad. I hate it! How do I stop?"

Discussion: Let's talk about that. How do we stop? (*Distinctly Different* has suggestions.)

Leader's Setup: Now back to Jabez. His biography is short and surprising. Read 1 Chronicles 4:9. Somehow Jabez decided, my life will not reflect what my mother gave me when she named me "Pain."

Jabez committed to this. A man whose family has known only despair can change the path for those who follow. Jabez did not pass on any pain he may have experienced.

When a person uses hurtful words they may be doing the same as Jabez' mother. She used a single *word* to communicate her pain. Unfortunately her *word* survived for decades to follow. Hurtful words are often not about the person to whom those words were spoken.

Discussion: Can you think of a man who broke the cycle of anger, addiction, laziness, prison his family had known? How did the man break that cycle?

Teaching Point: We do not choose our life experiences. We do choose our response to those experiences. Jabez' heritage and name expressed "pain." In spite of that heritage, Jabez's responded by being, "more honorable."

Imagine a man who has said, "I hate my father. He abandoned my mother and me when I was six years old." In time, that same man later abandoned his own family.

The boy abandoned by his father was an experience over which he had no control. The boy now becoming a man who later abandons his own family is a choice the man is making.

Jabez chose to be "more honorable."

The Hebrew word translated *honorable* in 1 Chronicles 4: 9, means "weighty or heavy." The same Hebrew word is at times used to speak of the "glory" of God. Jabez being honorable, meant he was influential. Jabez carried weight, not in the sense of physical weight, but with his impact on others. Jabez became a man of significance.

Discussion: What is it that makes a man more influential than some other man? (Some suggestions to possibly include; proper motivation; his life desires; is he diligent in his career; thoughtfulness, etc.)

Discussion: Now think about this, every man responds to life's pain in a different way. What ways have you seen men respond to pain? Why?

Leader's Setup: Contrast any of those with Jabez response to life. **And Jabez called on the God of Israel, . . .** (1 Chronicles 4:10) Jabez calling on the God of Israel indicated his priorities and approach to life.

Discussion: What would it look like for a man to consistently bring his disappointments, disappointments and "pain" to God?

Thoughtful Consideration and Application

1. What were the pain points of your young life? Perhaps your father was violent or verbally abusive. Maybe an older sibling caused pain. What is there about your life that you look back at and hate?

2. All men respond to their pain. You may respond in a different way than someone else, but we all respond to that pain. How have you coped with the difficulty life has brought to you?

3. What active steps will you take to protect future members of your family from the same pain that you suffered?

Session 6

God's Men – What Surrounds Does Not Define

Leader's Setup: We, men are surrounded! We are surrounded by a world filled with selfishness, pride, competitiveness and sensuality.

Discussion: *(This may be a discussion where you want to break the men into groups of 2, 3, or 4. It is best for every man to be involved.)* Think about work, high school and college: what has been the most Godless situation you ever faced? Why was that event a challenge for you?

Leader's Setup: Have someone read or tell the story of Gonzalo Guerrero found in *Distinctly Different*.

Discussion: Imagine a good friend being Gonzalo Guerrero. Can you envision the friend "going native?" Today's Christians live in a cultural and moral jungle. Apply the words "going native" to a Christian man becoming like the surrounding culture; what would his behavior be?

Leader's Setup: It is obvious that God's Men are to be *Distinctly Different*. <u>Have someone read Romans 12:2</u>. The Greek word translated, *conformed* means "to shape something by the use of a mold."

Discussion: Let's list some common characteristics of men who are not *Distinctly Different*? (<u>Note to leader:</u> Use a marker board or flip chart.)

Teaching Point: Do you see that these common traits are a result of being molded by the world system around us? To be "conformed" is to have the same world-view as your non-Christian neighbor or some man who is a nominal Christian.

Leader's Setup: Re-read Romans 12:2. Staying out of the world's mold required, "renewing the mind." A **_constant_** mental renewing produces a stubborn strength that resists the mold. Being squeezed into the world's mold shapes a man's thinking. If a man's mind is not renewed, he soon takes on the values and priorities of what surrounds him.

Being shaped into the world's mold does not happen overnight. Rather, it is a slow process of normalizing the abnormal. It goes something like this:

1. You hear a story that disrespects sexuality and turns women into a sex object. You are God-fearing. You don't even smile.

2. The barrage of such jokes and stories continues. In time, you laugh along with your fellow-workers.
3. How long before you tell the joke you heard at lunch to a group of men who have not yet heard it?

When the steps are complete the world system has reshaped the man. This molding happens regarding money, entertainment, sexuality, etc.

Discussion: Let's don't move away from this verse without thinking about mental renewal. What can a man do constantly to renew his mind? (Note to leader: *Distinctly Different* offers some suggestions. The men in your group will come up with others.)

Leader's Setup: John, who wrote the book of Revelation was on the island of Patmos. John was one of Jesus' earliest followers. John, may have been Jesus closest friend. After Jesus ascension, John had a productive ministry. Eventually, John was perceived as an enemy by the Roman government, who was the power of the day.

Discussion: Many countries have governments that are not an enemy of the church. The present opposition is more subtle <u>and also more significant</u>. On an almost daily basis, what are some of the things that oppose you being a man who is "Distinctly Different?" (After a bit have someone read Ephesians 6:12)

Leader's Setup: The principalities, powers, rulers of the darkness of this world, and spiritual wickedness in high places are aligned against you.

The strategy has not changed. Godliness must be eliminated or minimized. In the case of John, Rome planned to kill him or move him to a place where he could make no impact.

Briefly tell of the Emperor Domitian's attempt to kill John.

When Domitian could not destroy John, he isolated him on a prison island named Patmos. Read Revelation 1:9. On Patmos, John was surrounded by other prisoners.

John's companions likely included thieves, rapists and murderers. On Patmos John was immersed in a cesspool of vile men. You are not on a prison island, but often you are in similar filth.

Discussion: What do you suppose life would have been like on Patmos? Compare what was likely common on Patmos with John, the spirit-filled preacher. Do you suppose, Domitian thought that Patmos and its residents would change John?

Leader's Setup: (Note to the leader. There seems to be little way to get the following material in front of the group other than the leader providing it.) What Domitian was hoping to do to John, and what the world tries to do to God's Men is not unlike the conditioning practiced on captured soldiers during the Korean conflict of the 1950s. The approach became known as brainwashing.

The brainwashing technique resulted in a comparably higher percentage of American prisoners defecting to North Korea. When a cease-fire ended the hostilities, some American soldiers refused repatriation. Like Gonzalo Guerrero in 1519, these men were now content to live comfortably among people who were once their enemy. In some instances, such men joined the ranks of the North Koreans and Chinese fighting against South Korea and the United States.

In the spiritual realm this would be the equal of a once godly man changing his alliances. The man backslides, not only into sin, but into active opposition to Jesus' church. A man who does this has become apostate. The book of Jude has much to say about apostates.

The Chinese and North Korean "brain-washing" methods included:

1. Sleep deprivation. Tired men are dangerous. Modern man is over-committed.

2. Manipulation to break down the autonomy of individual thought. Such manipulation establishes the idea, "Everybody is doing it . . ."

3. To dehumanize men by keeping them in utter filth. The dehumanizing is mental, spiritual and emotional. Vulgarity is commonly heard from

educated and well-dressed people. God-ordered sexuality has become a marketplace of perversion. Men are "animalized."

4. Attacking a man's sense of self-identity. His life and decisions are not his own. Values have changed. That which was right is now wrong.

5. An incessant message that God's Men are wrong. In Korea, the loudspeakers in prisons blared, "You are wrong. Your country is wrong. You are guilty of crimes against humanity!" Every interrogation included the message. "You are wrong . . . your country is wrong!" The unceasing message to God's men is, "You are wrong." You are wrong if you don't drink. You are wrong if you think homosexuality is a sin! You are wrong if you attend church. You are wrong if you tithe."

Under such unceasing pressure men begin to think, "If I'm so different from everyone else, then surely something is wrong with me."

Discussion: Read 1 Corinthians 15:33. The words "evil communications" refers to *bad company.* Bad company ruins good manners. How have you seen the company a man keeps subtly brain-wash him into becoming like the people with whom he is spending time?

Leader's Setup: If a man lets the world determine his thought-life, he is doomed. Read 2 Corinthians 10:4-5.

Discussion: What do you consider the weapons of our warfare? How do you use those weapons?

Discussion: Notice, again Paul gives attention to the mind. He instructed: **bringing every thought into captivity to the obedience of Christ.** (2 Corinthians 10:5) Here is the hard part; how does a man bring his thoughts into captivity? *(Some ideas: he has to 'think about what he is thinking about, fill his mind with Godly goodness, when the wrong thoughts come to shoo them away.)*

Suggestion: There will be men in the group who are struggling. Their thoughts are seldom brought into captivity. It is a good time to pray for each other. Ask God to give men wisdom to know how to bring thoughts into captivity.

Thoughtful Consideration and Application

1. What most consistently challenges you in retaining the principles and behavior of a Godly man?

2. Have you watched a man who once worshiped with you, "go native?" What were the steps in the man losing his Christian identity?

3. How will you protect yourself from the same outcome?

Session 7

God's Men - In the Spirit . . .

Leader's Setup: We have talked about John being on Patmos. He would have been immersed in ungodliness. John overcame that challenge. In that session we focused on the first part of Revelation 1:9.

Read Revelation 1:9-10. **John was in the spirit on the Lord's Day.** Notice some things that did not cause John to be in the spirit:

- The revelation of Jesus Christ (Revelation 1:1) did not get John in the spirit.
- John was in the spirit <u>before</u> he heard a great voice (Revelation 1:10).
- The <u>surrounding environment</u> did not get John "in the spirit." What surrounded him would have been anti-godly.

Being "in the spirit" was an experience independent of John's location. Men can be, "in the spirit" wherever they are, and whatever the circumstance is powerful.

Discuss: what does it mean to be "in the Spirit? Read Romans 8:9. What does Romans 8:9 explain about the Spirit? (If needed: The word "dwell" indicates an abiding presence. To "dwell" is for the Spirit of God to take up permanent residence.)

Teaching Point: To overcome the surrounding pressure, Christian men must have God's spirit abiding within.

Discussion: The outpouring of the spirit on "whosoever will" is reported in Acts 2:1-4. (Have someone read the verses.) Those of you who know a bit about the Bible remind us of the things that preceded the events found in Acts 2:1-4.

Why were those things important? (*Distinctly Different* offers some insight if your group does not provide enough. Prayer was important. It preceded the group being filled with the spirit.)

Leader's Setup: Read Acts 4:15-18. Soon, the young church found themselves being persecuted. Peter and John were warned to do no more teaching or preaching in the name of Jesus.

When the two men told the group what had been done, the group responded with prayer. Read Acts 4:31. See how victory comes? Men who want to be "in the spirit," are men much in prayer. Patmos could not stop John from praying. John was in the spirit!

There is not a stressful situation that can keep a man from prayer.

Leader's Setup: Even before Patmos, John was a proponent of prayer. Read 1 John 5:14-15. John had been in the prayer meeting before the spirit was poured out in Acts 2. Sixty years later he was advocating for prayer.

Discussion: What are practical ways you use to be a "man of prayer?"

Leader's Setup: Being in the spirit requires prayer. There are also some behaviors a man must exclude if he wants to be filled with the spirit. Read Ephesians 5:18. Paul offered a contrast: "be not" and a "but be."

To be filled with the spirit, which is likely a synonym for being "in the spirit" a man must not be full of *other* things. While Paul warned about wine, many other things displace the spirit.

Discussion: What are some things men need to have on their, "be not" list? (As in "be not drunk with wine . . ..)

Leader's Setup: Let's turn this positive. Read Ephesians 5:19-20. Paul's list of behaviors that welcome the spirit to dwell within: (1) Speak to yourselves in psalms . . .. Paul's remedy included, "talk to yourself." (2)

Sing and make melody in your heart to the Lord. The singing is to be within. (3) Giving thanks always.

Discussion: How many people have to be present to practice any of the things mentioned in Ephesians 5:19-20. (This will be a short discussion. The answer is "one.")

Teaching Opportunity: Before Acts 2, John had joined others in corporate prayer. On Patmos, John was alone. John chose to behave in a way that allowed him to be "in the spirit on the Lord's Day . . .." Whatever your personal Patmos, you can also be "in the spirit."

Leader's Setup: If you know someone similar to V.C. Etheridge mentioned in *Distinctly Different* then use the man's story. Otherwise use the illustration about V.C. found in *Distinctly Different*.

Discussion: Is there someone you know who seemed to always be "in the spirit?" Can you identify any consistent behavior that made this possible?

Discussion: What would need to change in your own life to be like the men of whom we have just spoken? Men who were "in the spirit?"

Thoughtful Consideration and Application

1. What we put into our mind affects us. What do you listen to as you travel to work?

2. Do you think hearing more preaching or listening to an audio Bible would help you stay "in the Spirit?"

3. What is your prayer habit? If you don't have a prayer habit, it is unlikely you can stay in the spirit.

Other Material by Carlton L. Coon Sr. is available at CarltonCoonsr.com

Distinctly Different is the first in a series of books focused on the needs of Christian men.

Twitter: @carltonlcoonsr

Public Figure Facebook – Carlton Coon Sr.

Email: CarltonCoonSr@gmail.com

Made in the USA
Middletown, DE
21 March 2023

27279057R00024